1800 Indigo House
Excerpts of a life

The Poetic life
Of
Elaine Freeman-Anderson

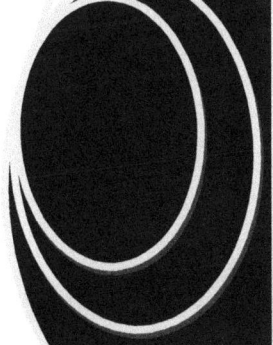

Naiobi's Designs and Publishing
Philadelphia, PA 19138-1422

1800 Indigo House Excerpts from a Life is the poetry of
Elaine Freeman-Anderson
Copyright °2007 by Elaine Freeman-Anderson
978-0-6151-5174-8
Publication Date: 2007-10-27
CID 78511

All writes reserved. Printed in the United States of America, no part of the book may be used or reproduced in any manner whatsoever without written permission.

Book Design by Elaine Freeman-Anderson

This Book is dedicated to my family who I love very much.

Thanks to *Shamika Elaine Freeman* my special proofreader and granddaughter. Who took out the time to read and give me her opinion? It inspired me greatly.

The Presence Within

In this house am I, the deepest presence created,
Learning and burning with loves essence and influence
Yet, I am humble of the power I possess,
Still I find that my house filled with the Great Spirit,
Who creates on so many levels?
Taking away my apprehension,
Building my self-esteem,
A realization, that I can give hope, happiness and myself
and never feel alone.

Introduction

In North Philadelphia in 1950 a year that most family structures were trying to stay together we were apart of the great migration from South Carolina to Washington, DC. In this Indigo House, a three-story row was the memories of a little girl who is now a woman of in her early fifties; she grew up with a family structure that was very loving. There were wonderful things that happen and deep lessons to learn. Yet, she found reflection on this time, she was apart of abuse, recognize that some of the feelings of unhappiness and caution were from the past. Through poetry, she was able to purge some of that hurt and pain that she experienced while growing up.

List of Illustration

The illustration Designs that appears in this work are created by
Elaine Freeman-Anderson

Baby Cries

Filipino Heroin Queen

Music Sheet of Trees

Grey Eyes

Spiritual

Hustler female

Table of Contents

Introduction	4
Excerpt:	10
Baby Cries	12
Grandpa Charles	13
The 1800 Indigo House	15
Papa Louis	16
Read me a Story before bed	17
Fannie Don't play…	18
Excerpts:	19
Spoiled little Girl	20
Excerpt:	21
Holy Spirit	22
Momma Returns	23
Excerpt:	24
The Drowning	25
Excerpt:	26
Rocking	27
Excerpt:	28
Who is this?	29
Excerpt:	30
I Don't Live Here Do I?	31
The devil tried to get me….	32
Excerpt:	33
"Abuse of two year old…."	34
Excerpt:	35
Scary	36
The situation	37

Table of Contents cont

Excerpt	38
Limousine Line	39
The Next Phase	40
Mom & Me	41
Just us	42
A forbidden Pastry	43
Excerpt:	44
Moses was his name…	45
My step Brother tried to kill me	46
Excerpts:	47
Two Men	48
Excerpt:	49
Seizures	50
Rent a TV	53
Excerpt:	54
Hand made quilts	55
The Seal	56
Phase II	57
Barefeet Summer	59
D.B. A spiritual friend	60
Living in fear	61
Riot	62
Skinny	63
Inside My Head	64
Excerpt:	65
The Nickel	66
Alcoholic Stroll	67
Maryland visited	68
A Southern Experience	69
Struggle	70
Silence	71
Experiencing a Murder	72
Golden Honey with Bees	73
My Dream	74

Table of Contents

Phase III	75
Weird Girl	76
The Madam of the house	77
Filipino Heroin Queen	79
Hippy	80
Drugs	81
The Number House	82
Orlando	83
Cousin Billy P.	85
Latin Jingo	86
Excerpt:	87
The Blackness of Amos	88
Excerpt:	89
Warriors of the Neighborhood	91
House of Females	92
Demarco	93
School Walkout	94
Excerpt	95
Love abuse	96
Teenage Mother	97
Hooky School	99
Discovery	100
Aunt Sister	101
Excerpt:	102
Grey Eyes	103
Driven	105
Homeless	106
A Extensive and Sandy Path	107
Nina	108
Excerpt:	109
Project living	110
Hustler female	113
Excerpt:	114

Table of Contents

No Food Just mouths _____ 115
East River Drive _____ 116
Holiday Nightmares _____ 117
Dark Stairway _____ 118
Haven _____ 119
Excerpt: _____ 120
Oboe _____ 121
Piccadilly _____ 122
Excerpt the Evaluation _____ 123

Excerpt:

Living in Washington DC my mother and father separated and she was left with a small baby, hurt and alone she could not sit still, it was the call of the wild. She had to get out of the house so she left me, with an elderly lady who for all tense and purposes was sickly and could not cater to a small baby girl. My mother did not return for quite a while and it left the drastic move of calling my grandmother who traveled from Philadelphia to Washington and retrieve me and I became her baby. I was rescued in 1950.

Baby gan ma

Baby Cries

An Eighty five year old lady
Cuddles a beautiful baby girl,
She calls for her momma,
It has been two weeks,
Nevertheless, she has not come back,
Mom, mom, mom, the sound of her cries
Not satisfaction of a bottle
No changing of the diaper,
The door opens,
Her little eyes peek from the side,
Not momma,
It's mom-mom.

Grandpa Charles

A mystic dream appear in my mind,

The scent of a pipe and the face

Of a man, that was the original,

Isn't it strange that I can remember your adore,

Yet in the room rocking me in your lap,

I reached with petite fingers to grab

The pipe until this day a scent,

That I really love. You passed away,

Papa Charles,

I just want you to know

That my heart

Belongs to you,

You are the original,

The first …

Excerpt:

When I was a baby, I lived on a block of row houses in an apartment on the third floor. The house unique bright blue you could not miss, and it was 1953. My grandmother Fannie lived here with my grandfather Louis who I adored. The block was huge and across the street were an equal amount of homes. Fannie saved my life.

The 1800 Indigo House

Colonial Row centered,
Three stories high,
Unusual soothing indigo,
Concrete blossoms
Bordering the Ceil,
A babe exist here,
A daughter
Granddaughter,
Our proprietor a Doctor,
Whose flat was at the first floor?
The measles stopover here,
My grandmother thrashes my mother here,
My spirit ran from solitary space to another,
I share the ball game with Grand pop, twisting his locks,
I drank my first beer here,
Snapping petite fingers without a thud,
Grandma gave me her last words here,
Then she went away,
The indigo house died from a wrecked spirit
It did not have the adore of our family,
So they tore it down.

Papa Louis

You save my life, fetch to Philly,
To a location that is safe,
Adorable sox and dresses you gave,
Forever keeping me secure,
Taking me with my wide mouth,
Never keeping a secret,
Always telling something that's right,
Baby sitting my littleness,
Experiencing the taste of ballentine and Shaffer,
Teaching me how to pop my finger,
Never in all the time that
You were my second grandpop,
You never raised your voice,
Or ever had to spank me,
Even when my comb was stuck in
Your noggin,
You were always a man of independent
Needs
Teaching about the thoughts of a man
He must make his own work,
Like you Grandpa Louis,
You have always made your own way,

Read me a Story before bed

Granny every evening joins me on bended knee,
To pray that special prayer,
Now I lay me down,
Then she settles me in to a cool pad,
I talked to her endless, asking questions,
She took out the only book that would
Shape my life,
The holy story, the original, not the revised,
The new without the old,
Not the one without Tobit,
And Enoch, it was revelation,
Visions of the twelve,
The history of our family was there,
Then she wanted me to understand the rules,
She read the Wisdom of Solomon,
And reasoning of Proverbs,
Then I would fall asleep,
Putting together a different me.
One, with love, hope, and happiness.

Fannie don't play...

My grandfather liked to chat on the phone,
A notion of a playa
Not a connoisseur
Don't call your other woman
From your house,
Don't take your granddaughter to
The other woman's house,
The tattletale,
Will tell,
Granny request grandpa to hang up
Thrice,
Its 1953,
Phones were weighty,
She stroll pass leisurely,
Grabbing its base
Crashing it side his mind
That was the first time that
Grandpa was at a lost for words,
I think it was brain damage.

Excerpts:

My grandmother would move mountains for me, yet I would test her patience beyond any child. My requests were beyond anything a person could think of but she did not want me to do without anything. So when she left I suffered so deeply because I have never been loved so much by anyone that way.

Spoiled little Girl

Pealing every grape of concord

Appeasing my heart,

Stressing her nerves

Unknowing of my request,

All she knew was her love,

Someday she wanted to,

Spank my tail,

Others I was the love of

Her life,

Nana little baby,

When awake rotten fruit,

When asleep a pure strawberry,

Granny flawed the little girl.

Excerpt:

My grandmother attended church faithfully she would quite naturally as all grandmothers did take their grandchild to church. It is when you want that child to know whom the higher power is, something's are strange to the young and so our reaction is not quite, what is expected. Our church was jam packed, people side by side and ushers standing in the floor, as the minister preached a sermon so deep that it moved everyone in so many ways. There was power in that room; there were rejoicing in that space. Sometimes something ugly was in that room. No matter who was in that room as long as I was with Fannie, there was love in that room.

Holy Spirit

She leaped from the hardness,
Of Pew seats,
Lifts her hands, blaring
In tongs they say,
Because of the power she felt,
Rolling in the isles,
The ushers came,
It was a message from a spirit,
Some say,
Others were in disbelief
Her actions were not of
A lady,
Flouncing for all to see,
Judgments of the parishioners,
Inquiry of her beliefs,
Ashamed with head hung low
She sat in a corner,
I felt envious of her.

Momma Returns

Concealed in the dimness, a half moon glow expose the face
of a woman, who came to see her mother,
Her baby revealed her,
Station almost in distress, she detect her mothers facial form
so well concealed, but to a baby girl it was divulge by the
spirits,
The dashing of Granny to see what a diminutive one cried out,
The invitation in the form of a shout for her immediate
presence before her majesty, climbing unhurried toward the
thrashing that she so deserve for her actions
Lashing out toward her as she came upon the final stair,
Momma please let me explain, but there was no justification
for ditching your infant,
Granny reclaims her desired strap, and whips my momma with
her sturdy appendage,
Tears from eyes and screams from my lips,
Please mom, mom, don't beat Mommie!
And the onslaught continued,
Until finally grandpop emerges to saves me from the theatre
of pain.

Excerpt:

My grandmother thought that her way to protect me is to make sure that I was always in the company of the master. So she decided when she joined another church that she would just take me to be baptized. In the ninety fifties they could baptize you in so many ways. I was not aware of that ritual believe me, they would have to find another way to do that too me.

The Drowning

Coming round the corner,
Leaning against a
Whitewashed building,
A warped unlock door,
There was a gathering,
Of elderly and youthful,
Standing in line,
Anticipating an unusual
Ritual, singing, praying
Were they?
All I wanted to do is play,
We came to the door,
Our feet step inside,
A barrel of water filled,
The old man with a robe
Held a black book in his left,
His other brown hand,
Pushed her head down
Deep and held it there,
I took off,
They ain't gonna drown me.

Excerpt:

I was fearless, exhibiting myself for all to see. Just that morning I begged her to let me wear my Easter clothes.
"No you can't because they are special occasions."
I cried myself to sleep because I could not have my way.

Rocking

Presume asleep, I awaken,
Discovering, no one home,
Amusing myself, a closet,
Easter dress on backwards
Shoes on the wrong foot,
Hat on hanging on the side,
Perched myself on the third floor ceil,
For all to admire,
Rocking to Sam Cooke,
My mother who was eight- point-
Five months pregnant,
Observe her baby rocking back and forth,
Plummeting groceries kiss the earth, sprint
Two flights and
Grabbed my stupidness,
Arms embrace me,
Lack of breath featuring fear,
Instantly and devoid of warning
Was the blazing bottom?
What I thought?

Excerpt:

My mother comes home to her abandon child only because once again she was pregnant. My little sister was a surprise; she was hiding this little person all that time. Finally, I guess they decided to spring my new sibling on me. Big mistake, because I was not having it no kind of way.

Who is this?

Waking up to Max the coffee, I knew that my Granny was home. A sound of someone else was here, place upon the edge of the sofa was a baby girl. She was brown, round and she kicks, coos and sucks on her hands, my Granny is playing with her.

The burning feeling of hurt brought questions from lips, inquiries of what, who and how long would she be here. My eyes watched her closely and my mind wanted to inform her that this was my Granny, and this baby's presence is not wanted.

She smiled and coos as if all I said was irrelevant to her. She had no care of my being in the same room; I did not understand her world I had never been taught.

Brown baby disappeared from my granny's house, next time she appeared, I tried to make her disappear, only two years old.

Excerpt:

A small child's mind is very active and they can comprehend knowledge well. My grandmother had a way of bringing her point home. She knew my mind, that's and Aquarian for you Loving and Deep.

I Don't Live Here Do I?

Momma tried to be slick,
She moves in a new place,
She tried to move me in this place
Its time to go home I say,
I been here all day,
Where is my mom-mom?
She better come and get me, today,
I cried and begged,
Begged and cried,
This isn't my room,
I want to go home soon,
This is your home baby,
You will see mom-mom tomorrow,
I stomp and scream
And hollered as loud as I could
In through the door,
Twelve midnight,
In darkness of night, without a fight,
Baby you gonna have to stay with your Momma,
No mom-mom I want to go home with you,
Mom-Mom whispered, this your fault,
You abandoned her,
She doesn't trust you.

The devil tried to get me....

I had tested my nanas serenity,
To the end and she was
Truly weary of my attitude,
She had no problem in
Whipping the brownness off you
If necessary,
After my well defined behind whipping,
I went to sleep,
The last thing my grandmother said to me,
The devil is hiding in the corner laughing at you,
Of course I tried to see him but he did not
Manifest,
Once I shut my eyes I was off to nap with my spanking,
Well guess who was waiting for me, once I was in dreamland
The Devil, I watch him and he was coming after me.
Relentless, amused,
How does he look? You ask,
No idea,
Waking up, just in time.

Excerpt:

My mother and grandmother had to work because in the fifties if you did not work then you would starve and be homeless or as my mother said, you would be in the poor house. Therefore, my mother would take me to a baby sitter a very nasty hateful woman. She lived in house with twenty kids and I was the only outsider. She was dark skinned and she did not like light skinned people, for some reason she was under the impression that we thought, we were cute. What bothered me was why you would baby-sit for someone that you do not like. Oh, that is right, the money, and you can get to torture their kid all you want.

"Abuse of two year old...."

Little girl of abuse,
There were all kinds
Defined by the abusers
The mother,
The babysitter who dangled the petite person,
By one foot and thrashes her,
Because she peed in the floor,
It was their Fault,
Lock the toilet
Ignored pleases to let me in,
Moisture uncontrolled streams
Down slender limbs,
Scared of the consequence,
An enormous woman,
Who did not like the child anyway?
Raise a belt slamming against her
Small being, face, arms, legs without
Prejudice, until she was out of breath,
A yella girl and her yella momma,
Beating, screaming raging
Didn't I tell you not to pee on yourself?
The narrative changes
Huge babysitters little angry daughter,
Sever the top dreadlock,
Attempt to plant it on her head,
My mother realize a missing lock,
Napping my eyes saw scissors,
Two years old if that,
Saved, from the beater.

Excerpt:

On that block with the indigo house I often was told to sit on the steps and do not go anywhere, but I was going to learn a valuable lesson Listen to my family because you can get in a lot of trouble.

Scary

I considered myself
An explorer,
Seeking out spaces,
Unknown adventures,
Entering structures,
Where the gate locks,
No escape insight,
Calls my protector
Momma I utter,
Fear brought tears,
At last, somebody found me
Slumbering in the foyer,
My carcass materialize outside
The entire police force,
Was at my front entrance,
Among my mother,
Grandmother
Grandpa,
And host of other well known,
Friends and relatives,
Celebrated for a brief moment,
I will by no means do that again.

My own spanking…

The situation

Apart of something I can't describe
All I know that it was practiced in Africa,
When a woman can't conceive
Then he must find one who can

But

The arrow pierces his heart
And we lived there
In this situation
We shared her love
She shared he knowledge
We shared our youth
She shared her time

But

All the time she was in pain,
Because she could not conceive
And she had to share with another.

Excerpt:

In my family to be, an Eastern Star in that early time was a pillar, and there were privileges to being in that time that place. We road in the limousines to church on special occasions, and I would accompany Fannie were ever she went. It was that last time that the limousines visited and I guess I just did not like them ever since. There was a sense of betrayal there.

Limousine Line

I peaked through the window,
Line black Limousines,
Church cars that escort,
Injured within a forgotten me,
Tear encompass my eyes,
They would not allow me beyond,
Held in reserve,
They did not want me to discern,
It was Granny's last journey,
Ripped from my heart,
Reminiscent of something missing,
The one time I lost your apron string,
The one time I was not under foot,
Unable to be your shadow,
Called away,
You will revisit
Isn't that funny,
Isn't that like…?

The Next Phase

We moved out that Indigo three-story house, it was heart breaking to leave a place were I had so much love given to me.

My mother sat by the window, with a look of puzzlement in her eyes, her mother was gone and she did not know what to do. The deep pain that she was experiencing did not have anything to do with me.

My mother sat in the dark of a living room that she shared with her mother waiting and hoping that her spirit would appear; obviously, she did not want to visit my mother, because she did not want to appear.

Not wanting to sit still at the tender age of three, I played in the living room just mom and I, scared of the boogieman; I stared down the hall to see my Granny appear coming into the front room.

"Grandmom!" As quickly as the image stood before me in the dark hall, when I looked again she was gone. My mother leaps from her chair and stares.

"Where?" She screamed crashing her knees against the hard linoleum.

"Why she won't come to me?" My mom's moans and cries echoed through the half empty apartment.
"Don't Cry Mommie she will be back."

Mom & Me

A team we are, trying to help each other

Best we can,

Elevated to the top of a chair

Learning to iron

Pressing the skirt,

Then the collar,

Hurry baby we have to go soon,

A bond between us,

A one-room place over top

Of an eye glass place,

Marble steps, I play, this was to me

A happy place, no pain, No confusion,

Just mommy and me working

Our thing together,

She needed me,

Like I needed her,

Just us

I was momma's partner,
Counselor and best buddy,
She would gossip about the people in
Juice joint.
Laughter generated from the house,
Sometimes I accompanied mom,
When everyone was feeling no pain,
They would place my small frame on a coffee table
I would sing,
Shaw, Shaw the moon,
Jiggling coins from my audience
Well hidden in my little red Dress coat
Pocket,
You have money,
I think you did it girl,
You are a star.

A forbidden Pastry

Summer day a little frame
Descends outside,
Down mason stairs
A Corner apothecary,
Sitting on the steps,
Eyes see around the corner,
A bag neatly packaged,
For inquisitive eyes,
A sweet potato pie,
Munching quickly,
And sneaking back inside,
Man looking for his pie,
Where could it be?
Who would of known?

Excerpt:

The early years of my life were of inquiry, living with my mother who needed someone to talk to, she made me her confidant. Never think that your young one does not understand what is going on. When you are in an abusive relationship they know the cost and pain, if you ask them what they think, people would say lets get away from here; this is not where I want to be.

Moses was his name...

A woman's significant other,
An abusive man who griped his women,
With a iron will,
He kept all of them under control,
A little girl of two-experience life in
A grown up way,
Orchestrated abuse to her mom
Threats with words, hands extended
In the air, man of disrespect,
Gathering his outside woman and parading her
Before his wife, to extract his son, coaching his way,
There were ten siblings like him,
He never paid any attention,
Demanded his girlfriend's presence and to bring
Her little one that was two,
Warning about her hesitation, that he would
Show his force before all,
The two women situated before each other,
The wife defiant, her son stays,
Of course he still ruled that house too.
Intimidation clearly brings his words to reality,
You know what I will do to you...
I have no qualms about it...
Do not let my girlfriend see you get your ass whipped.
Both women had tears, but the wife complies,

My step Brother tried to kill me

Calm it was night,
My remains lay upon a cot,
My sister and myself at the base,
And my stepbrother at the summit,
While our parents were next door
At the juice joint,
Determined with lit candles,
The game
Placing them in the hole
Penetrating a cot,
Then we slept,
Awaken by a firefighter,
The apartment a blaze,
Needless to say
We did not see
My stepbrother
Anymore.

Excerpts:

The decision of a woman to have a lover in there life isn't really hard it is just that when that lover is an abusive and that person decides to leave that is when the struggle begins. The scene was reminiscent of when Solomon had to make the decision of who would get the baby. So did the little one who came to the aid of her mother, because ultimately neither one had any rights.

Two Men

Vying for her attention,
She only wants one,
They fight with a knife,
The other wants to cut her in half,
The daughter runs to the kitchen,
Grabs her knife,
Coming into the room,
Stop!
Let her go, she my Mommie,
Neither of you can have her,
She belongs to me,
They stopped in disbelief,
Raising up,
Turning to her,
Who do you want?

Excerpt:

This was also a time of turmoil for a mother, who had tried to show that she could be a good mother,
When her baby girl had problems mentally because she had been injured she fell and hit her head. She never perceives the world from that spectrum of reality anymore. She has visitors who travel to her inner knowledge with scary thoughts, like the boogieman who constantly harass you with visions of your demise only to find that he can't do anything to you. That it is important to take back what belongs to you. Sometimes you are in another world for days one that no one but you can see. Suddenly you are in a hospital getting your fingers pricked. Query of feeling that you only just now began to feel, but you try to remember that your soul is here on earth and you are suppose to be visiting reality. . My mother was constantly in hospital corridors trying to bring me back, and sometimes I would be gone for days and just sudden as I left guest what I'm back. My poor mother stressed to limit because she can't get a real answer to my dilemma. It's of course 1953.

Seizures

A lock box soul who can't get out is hearing the sound of a monster chasing me. He sends in the sound of a black wagon of death to retrieve me from life, but I fight his take over with thoughts of being with my mom.

So many times I lay me down to sleep and awaken three days later or more, journey to a time and place until this day is s blur, who are you with loudness of voice in my head?

When you stop torturing me, what did I do to you? I can hear the horses galloping and the wagon attach cracking the whip, smack, yes they are almost here at my bedside. Coming steadily, consistently to stop me from breathing, living and sharing my softness with those who occupy this space. But soon a savior comes to rescue me, and I listen, hear his voice saying this is the truth, I will help, and you are my friend.

I'm an old Soul

A speak easy not a calm place, Saturday sunrise
Ms Gina was pleasant lady,
Festive house, drawing souls in concert
Amused and merriment,
I had to scurry over to our dwelling
Adjacent to that domicile and errand to retrieve
For momma
Running up the steps,
Precise throughout the vestibule,
To an extensive corridor, pressed the gate open
Swiftly someone captures me,
It was Moses,
A knife to presses my neckline,
He sought momma, elicited my help,
Keep him a secret,
Don't tell her he is in wait,
But soon as he released me,
Pumping heart, and petite limbs,
I ran with words forced from my
Hostage throat, warning momma,
The man seizes him, an authority,
Did he assume my compliance?
To use a weapon of slaughter
Then he is not aware of an old soul.

Excerpt:

We had the first rental television. It was box black and white that had a coin slot that took only nickels. Ten nickels inserted into a box attached to the picture tube. Image just when you are looking at an exciting scene in a soap opera the television just shuts off. Oh shh!

Rent a TV

Momma's only luxury, a TV,
Glue to the soap,
Mayta husband is devious,
The secret is revealed momma waited all
Weekend to see the final cut,
She made sure her work is done,
She warned me to be quiet,
Then the scene is on,
Momma's face so focused,
Sweaty palms, while feet planted firmly
On the floorboards,
Then just as the husband is caught
The TV screen turns black,
More money please,
                    Momma scrambles to insert nickels,
                          Klink, Klink, Klink zip,
                              It was the 1954
                      When the television returns
                        The commercial was on,
                          Our first rented TV.

Excerpt:

Sunday evenings while watching television my mother's job was to create blankets, because she did not have the money to buy them. Unique was this woman; she had a plan for whatever you wanted to do. In the 1960s she would look at the apartment and say we are going to paper these walls or paint the baseboards. We had a new apartment every year. We put down linoleum floors or reupholstered kitchen chair with oilcloth. Amazing!

Hand made quilts

Seated upon the bed removing buttons

Of pearl and plastic,

From dresses and shirts that grace my being,

Taking scissors she cuts fabric,

Square pieces and places them in a sack,

My sister and I seated upon linoleum and

Watch television as she creates

Quilts by hand,

Narration of me covers of warmth,

Seersucker, cotton plaid, I commit to memory,

It was my favorite shorts,

A shirt that fit for so long,

But then a piece never worn,

And then my sister remembers,

"That belongs to me,"

        On a cold winter's night, we have more than one,

            My mother has one for her couch,

              I wonder what she did with them.

The Seal

Upon the crown is a seal,

Keeping all in

Knowledge was limited,

An insignia, being saved, Born Again,

Only by thee,

A Query must enter, a inspiration requests

A way out,

                                        The emblem became solid,

                               Insanity was created on the right of

                                                The crown,

The query could not enter the left of reality,

There is no explanation,

No creation,

Who is he with symbol on the intellect?

Your days are numbered,

What is your glory?

Phase II

The *1960's* were the best times for me and then again it was the worst. Here is when you are about to move into apartment that is absolutely beautiful the year looks like something out of house and garden. The wide-angle streets were lined with beautiful three story homes. Our block was kept absolutely cleaned. Music, neighbors and respect were still in tact then, Life as young child then were so easy and quiet. The sun would beam down on street paved so neatly; neighborhood sanitation trucks were very diligent in their endeavors to keep everything sparkling. The milkman delivered milk and sometimes bread.

On Sunday morning, the paper man would shout throughout the streets "Inquirer" and I would rush down to the steps to greet him with my five cents for a massive amount of paper with cartoons and other goodies. Gospel time roared from open window as Louise would bless our neighborhoods and then she would put the Dixie hummingbirds, or James Cleveland to sing to us about love of a spiritual entity. My mother's favorite

"A long and dusty road."

Louise said I don't know what kind of trouble you are in or what is bothering you in your life, but I hope listening to the piece will help you make it through your day.

Barefeet Summer

Summer in the city
A vigil of going to the store,
A pack of cigarettes
A loaf of bread
Daily news,
And a five-pound bag of sugar,
All out of a dollar
Just fifteen cents change
Barefeet skip pass pebbles
To hurry back home,
Hoping they let you keep the
Change,
Young feet touching the bare heat,
A country girl,
Without sneaks,
Friends in Unisys,
They too must travel that way,

Cute little
Tootsies
Brown, beige and blue,
The young colors of summer

D.B. A spiritual friend

A love in the neighborhood,
He long for my heart, his almadine smooth skin, and
Striking brown eyes had my heart, before the day of
tragedy,
He confess his love to me and I did not respond,

Within my existence he could have been the solitary
adore,
The single spirit that pursue me, guiding my feelings,
Before any of that could happen, others were massacred.

Then they linger patiently to pilfer my loves life, they
sent a spy, and a calm spirit, that levy his dealings and
forewarn him, yet he did not have time to heed.

He left me to retrieve his little sister, his footpath
mounts the spherical steps to the cathedral, and she sang
in a choir, he never made it to her, when a shadowy
spirit, snatches his verve, and seize it, leaving his final
expressions of love for his mother.

Living in fear

A monster came and lived with us,
Growling hatred, taking out his wicked
Ways upon us like we knew his secret,
Beating us whenever he felt the need,
Molesting us whenever his passion would arise,
A decision was made,
Express my interest, to give to his way,
Fear struck his heart,
Then he threw me away,
The monster was still among us,
Now he was molesting my sister,
I met him and caught him in the Act,
He continued who would know.
Who would care?
Scared to tell, what would be the consequence?
All would hate us.
The monster would continue.
One day the monster died and now we are safe.

Riot

Sitting on my steps at 1964, people marching toward
Columbia on the avenue, angry people wanting a different life,
Jewish shopkeepers,
Have no idea they are the targets of hatred,
Stores were looted, a neighborhood changed,
Upon shoulders men carry televisions that no one can claim.

Clothes for children that prices exceeded all the money that
Midas could touch. Bats of weapons that they must use to
make their point, the panther has flex its paws,

Martin has a peaceful way, but the community wants a change
more dark presence in places of authority, ownership of
business, create work for us, we are tired, our words will be
heard, no longer slaves to the master,

An uprising, there is civil unrest they report, a revolt like the
time of tea but not a party,
A rebellion, more understanding; now we have been heard.

Skinny

To thin to think, bones with skin,
Veins visible to the human eye,
Yet silky butterscotch,
Baby fine hairs emerging through
Radiant tanned skin,
My legs looked like baseball bats,
Never could see the beauty of me,
Always, self conscious,
The ugly duckling
Am I going to be a swan?
Skinny no shape
No boobs,
No butt,
Everything in a straight Line
Getting everything in place,
Then changing to something else.

Inside My Head

Never emerging into this world,
Outside a window I stand,
Watching the story play out,
An invisible love,
A feeling so deep,
Going out among the world,
Yet I was in another,
 Inside My intellect,
Visions of magnificent realms,
Great works of art I observe,
Wisdom among those I perceive,
This is my other world,
Trying hard to make it real
Magnificent pharaoh
An ancient love affair,
The setting of the moon,
The rising of two suns,
Orange water and
Artistic sky, the story is always of love

Excerpt:

There was a reverend that own a candy store and created a church on my block. Years had gone by and he literally begged me to join his church, I had been to many churches during my years as a child. My grandmother was an eastern star and she was on the board at her church. I think he found me at a vulnerable time and I gave in and attended one of his services.

Many of the children on the block saw me attend and we made a date to go the next Sunday After that the church was filled to capacity, and I stopped going. At first because I just became too lazy. I would see the reverend in the candy store, trading large soda bottles for five cents.

Imagine that your family had brought you up believing in god and the people in the church are the examples of god's people, and then you meet a minister who cheats little children out of pennies.

Can you imagine what thoughts that child must be having? Disillusioned by those who are in the hierarchy of the church? Really until this day I am suspect of many ministers. Not just because of the Reverend, but there have been others over time that have shown me reasons to not believe.

The Nickel

                      Reverend a teacher of the word,

                              Implored my presence,

                                   In his modest church,

                         A corner use to be a store,

                            Individual chairs with

                            No one but his family,

Why would he be amongst the

Representatives yet there

Was no one to council?

                                     Then the story is

                        Revealed, the trick, scam, cheated

              A modest child who did not tally his coins,

                              A man of renown,

                                  Lied to him,

                                  In front of me,

There was no nickel,

Beware mature ancestors,

Immature, observes,

For they are not judging,

They are in quest of truth

In you…

Alcoholic Stroll

Friday night a bottle of Seagram's Gin,

Fish, French Fries

Old Seventy-Eight Records

A history of Music taught,

Johnny Ace, Orioles,

Crying the Chapel,

Pledging my love,

Old people doing the Jitterbug,

And then the Bop,

To Smoky fully juiced,

The alcoholic stroll across the linoleum floor,

Parents a pair

Of lesson in life they gave,

A family cherishes moment.

Maryland visited

A trip of summer the four-hour bus rides,
Long distance, seeing cows and horses
And land as long as the eye can see,
Boats, and little houses standing alone,
With no one around,
Don't they see the bus of us?
Miles of wooded area,
I did not know exist what is out there in the
                                  Thicket of every tree,
                       The highway moving fast under
            The greyhound, stores with strange names,
Where are the people?
I only see them in cars,
Signs of Salisbury, Pocomoke,
We are almost there,
The motor is silent as it moves forward,
The people inside start to stir,
Little homes so beautiful stand alone,
This is what I want...
Smells of spring water in the air,
                    Strange tongs speaking of dirt dobbas
                          Yet a people of love
                          Embrace me like family
                              I miss them

A Southern Experience

     Grass as afar as the eye could see, forest of leaves clapping like an audience who welcomes me to Salisbury and Pocomoke, and lands of crops to be harvested. Corn fields are abundant, my being sprints to the end, a ravine, almost a plunge to my death,

     Row of bushes sat on edges of ditches with great crabs waiting for tender feet to invade the liquid. Red berries hold a secret, of its sweet essence, that mama Recee warns us not to partake, yet the secret is unveil the next sunlight, rashes that swathe my façade, leave embarrassed reaction, lonesome hours I tutor my being to ride a bike, fear is drown in my determination to go the distance.

     Mama's blueberry pies, hot and loving were topped with vanilla cream, unaware of its powerful goodness. The smell of the air kept my mind mesmerized by love, missing my momma only came when I was no longer around her, then comes Shalinda, Jackie, Katie and Ann to play little girls stuff.

     Foul smells of water that is brought from the springs; taste so good when creating ice tea. Family gave their love to me, embrace my love for them, I love Maryland, if I had to pick a place to lay down my life among the ancient African spirits who surrounds the lands then this is my place of serenity.

Struggle

Always in conflict with someone,
What is their reasoning?
Constantly finding motives to hate me,
Fabrication that I said, yet not,
So call deceitful friends,

Plot my demise,
Abhorrence for being me,
The world of neighborhood

Was not prejudice?
On the street, in school,
Over someone else's domicile,
This emotion causes introversion,
Not wanting to be apart of them,
Who judge, hate and discriminate?
For whatever their opinion,
Why me?

Silence

We traveled that day in the hot stillness to,
Vaux to learn sewing and cooking,
A different day,

                    Something unusual in the air we sewn our
                    Wrap around skirts and cut out shift dresses,
                    We are having English after lunch,

That day
A stop for a hoagie and soda,
To quench our thirsty throats,
From the humid heat, but my mind was aware of something sinister in the air,

Something we would not be aware,
Silence so deafening it burst my ears,
A death reported to us,

                    We must go straight home,
                    Someone has killed the president,
                    How could someone do that?
                    Why would someone kill?
                    That only happens in films,

Maybe it is a mistake,
Now my world will be
Forever changed to bring about reality,
A president,
 Can be assassinated.

Experiencing a Murder

Voice of Rage in the expanse from my windowpane,
I peeked to glimpse a woman, who was being abused by her mate,
Immature and terrified I view the whipping so merciless,
He yells flaming expressions of revulsion yet he presume to love her,
Hands thrashes and resonance of slaps with the equivalent response from the pain,
What could make a man so angry to place his hands upon a frail flower and obliterate it petals?
She was petrified,
She saw her existence perish before her and so in her defense,
She seizes an object and pierces his heart and he fell,
Immobile on the floor,
She weeps, because he has made her experience something
That she did not believe in,
Murder,
But he was going to slay her,
Yet they charged her anyway,
Setting her broken body behind bars,
And just like the count
They forgot her existence.

Golden Honey with Bees

Females of golden honey with voices of invention,
Their music was only fleeting,
They went into the house of the brothers of harmony,
One Bee fell deeply for that brother whose voices
The human race cherished, he was from the house of azure
interpretation, and I could not help but feel that he did not
have the approach she allege,
But who was I, an immature teenage girl, who sought after the
similar obsession,
To have the golden voice that brought people to my heart,
when I exchanged words of wisdom,
She said that I needed to be more focus,
Then she went away,
I never really heard from them again
No honey
And no bees

My Dream

A theatre in dark burgundy,
Rows of seats on the floor and balcony,
Curtains silk drawn closed to not reveal,
The gift of those, whose recordings are lost to me,
Designs so intricate in her, it was antique,
Standing on the stage
Was I singing the songs of great groups?
Written music of time of immense feelings
Of love of a girl for a guy and the other,
Betrayal was limited,
Yet, respect was foremost,
Groups of those who knew my feelings,
Who dance in unison, making their way?
Across the stage,
It was fourteen days of song,
And shows all day
It was my pleasure in life
To see those whose talents
Grace its uptown.

Phase III

My block was one of three-story brownstone row of all kinds of characters who had their way of life. We had a madam on the block that had a family of entrepreneurs and women of the evening. From time to time pimps would stop by to see how the ladies were doing, the expressway of love and as the madam ran it discreetly like an after hours spot.

The drugs were across the street, potent packages of heroin delivered by a man who never would drink liquor nor do drugs, but he had plenty of drugs to sell to the neighborhood right in the trunk of his brand new sports car. Those funny cigarettes had not quite caught on yet, but the scene would change again. We had the speakeasy, and number house, ran by a husband, wife and her mother, money is a plenty for illegal thoughts.

In my next lesson in this life that made me pay close attention to how, if you are beautiful light skinned young girl you could be caught up easily. I learned to keep my mouth shut and my ears alert and watch my step.

The madam tried to recruit me for the house and the drug dealer was trying to sell me some drugs. One thing about my block there was never a dull moment. If I had to do something illegal it would be a after hours spot, but none of that was very productive for me.

Weird Girl

A peculiar friend of mine
She was pallid and yet black
With numerous lovers,
Adolphous the Greek and Vincent an African King,
Two gangs they rivaled,
One shadowy and other illumination,
She could never remember their names,
Her motivation were their gifts,
Her specialty is intellectual adversity,
She practice it on them everyday,
They love it,
They threatened each other,
They fought each other
They would eradicate each other,
But they love her...

The Madam of the house

Her majesty lay out before everyone in her enormous divan.
She was massive like beluga, but her self-esteem made her a queen to all who crosses her corridor,
Hands extended, caressed and kissed by those who were familiar with her influence, features so supple and stunning as
Black curls bordered her façade, polished nails extended beyond the softness of her skin.
Her robes were satin colors of lavender, black and gold enclosed this life form who ruled her house with a iron hand,
be afraid, she said, be very afraid,
She charges fifteen dollars but they got seven fifty, and she took out insurance on all,
Burial insurance, and when they left the planet she buried them.
She ruled her husband and children,
Yes, they were a family business,
Of course, her daughter was never on the menu,
Her ladies were Gloria, Susan and Sherry, not the Catawba, whom infected her patrons with syphilis and gonorrhea a contribution that keeps on giving, so someone else could experience the delights of
The madam.
Madam Guest were pillars of the community who wish to indulge in these sorted pleasures,
Decades pass, generations manifest, but the madam,
Left the planet, I guess?

Filipino Heroin Queen

Facial appearance of a woman whose home originated in the Philippines, striking features and soft curly hair, aristocratic words designing a story of her journey to my land, she tells of the mistrust, but she bore one who inscribe harmony, and appreciated its art form so clear as the melody softly penetrated the flute,

Like an interview, I query her reasons for her addiction,
Why thirty years putting holes in her skin
Unable to find places to penetrate she advises me.

This is a trash, scraping from the bottom; only the pure could be found in the Philippines; a picture of her so beautiful, She laid the picture against her facade revealing her structure was changing to a deceased person and her time was limited, Yet she continued to peel open cellophane powder and heated the substance,
Laid out her works, she nicknames it.

As if a student inserted into a heroin class this queen brought forth knowledge, that if I strictly absorbed her words, I will gain knowledge of a drug and I would stay away. If not I would become a patron, Grateful of the spirits for assisting me, to glimpse the path.

Hippy

A Young and impressionable sister,
Who brought forth a son who she cherished?
The father was no longer in her life.
She loved him famously
Leaving a seed of a handsome baby boy in the mist made her the queen.
That peace would not be,
She was in the house of heroin,
People envied her lifestyle although She was not apart of it.
Addiction thieves came to heist.
Piercing a boy's heart with a bullet,
They committed matricide too.
Hippy transform to someone else
She started to partake
Of the influence
Of the demon heroin
A battle to kick at times.
Her only soothing recourse was the G clef
Music notes of pain that she wrote between lines.
Just like Pan, she played the flute

Drugs

The fiend of odium
A terror chronicle
A Lie it informs you,
Someday drugs,
Will be an audition,
You will discern just
Who he is…

The Number House

Laughter from those, whose verse is a sexy lingo,
Drink was dark brown liquor,
The choice of those who wanted to reach a certain high, play
me a three for fifty cents, a voice carried
Familiar with that calculation, I cannot hit anything
Except this bottle in front of me,
People sitting around a kitchen table working it out,
They are the ones who is quiet as it's kept,
Pay me my money Ruby enters in stiletto heels, and a
Draped mink coat, I hit that four eight two for ten
Don't touch my money if you can't count!

Orlando

A West Indian Man, his age was of no value to me,
His accent intrigued me,
I was his baby queen,
He wanted my sex, yet I was a virgin to his mind,
Never asked any questions of him,
Just wanted to be in his presence,
Wanted to travel to a place of happiness,
Candle light dinners at the wagon wheel,
Drinks and then home,
Never did I query his intentions
My man from Trinidad,
Aware of my age he knew that I was his one,
But he betrays me,
Married to his wife and sex with my girlfriend,
He realize his mistake,
And begs me back
Orlando,
My heartthrob from Trinidad.
We can never dance again.

Cousin Billy P.

Deep, intense words, a poet who penetrated my being
Was someone my family had part of its design,
I listen to his music and his fame,
Something he was not ashamed,
His demeanor was silky
Jazz on a sailboat of a starry evening,
His orifice made me envision a crooning
I met his suave and sophisticated
Scats of Ella and Nina while Miles
Infiltrated for a moment,
Nineteen seventy when,
He was just the powerful Beginning,
I was proud to be apart of him
I a poet, he a singer,
I wish that he would sing poetry to me,
That he wrote on thin sheets of trees.

Latin Jingo

The razor sharp sound of a high-strung guitar, the thumping heart Retort almost naturally while sitting in a Lincoln Town Car,
The beauty encompass my spirit,
Who is this that penetrates my being,
Leaving a flaming emotion in a night of summer heat,
Latin drums could be heard throughout,
A new jingo educating my mind,
My universe is opened to me
Heaven is being taught,
A spiritual Manifestation leads
Me into a promiscuous thought
Closing my eyes taking in the power
Of rhythms that surround me,
Give me your love, play my life form
With every clef a sign of a beautiful staff,
Reminding me of jungles of the Amazon,
Notes of measure traveling through exotic places in my psyche,
All I see is Jingo

Excerpt:

Everyone who lives on the same block knew each other. Everyone did not take all things so serious at least those with a pure heart and the alcoholics, I remember the men of renown who influence the neighborhood. Mr. Kelly brought the children ice cream, Mr. Oliver took us on trips, and Mr. Amos he gave us comedy. We lived on a block that had houses on both sides of a large street. We called the old people nosey but they looked out for us. There was no problem for a parent to get into an argument about her children. We had the bakery on the corner, the apothecary who could put together caster oil with the quickness. The cleaners on the hill I lived for the fresh hoagies made by Ida's Restaurant.

The Blackness of Amos

Little people playing hopscotch
On marble steps Girls
Playing jacks, little boys play marbles,
A summer day,
The heat is present in the air
Everyone is having fun,
People are wandering from solitary dwelling to another,
A classic Saturday,
An accent in remoteness,
A lofty vague silhouette his darkness is of ancient Africa,
His dental ware is white as the driven snow,
His beam was immense,
What are you laughing at? Do not laugh at Mr. Amos,
I just full of juice

Delores approach

Help me I cannot make it
She peeks from her entry, shaking her head,
Oh Mr. Amos you in trouble,
He places his forefinger in front of his face,
Never touches his lips,
Shh! He utters, she will not let me in,
Stumbling up the steps, Delores soft
Spoken manner would encourage him to come in,
I told you about drinking without something to eat.
Yes, honey your right,
I am going straight to bed,
He turns and winks his eye at us,

We just giggle.

That was Mr. Amos.

Excerpt:

"Watching young men from gangs bond together to have a show of force in the neighborhood." Many are lead by misguided ideals. All they hear is the message in their minds and the feelings in their soul saying that he must go on the hunt."

I watch many of my friends die because of those ideas, but how can you fight yourself. These young powerful entities must follow what they feel. Now in the 1960, many men could not be the kind of man they wanted to be because of the system that was in place in our community.

Sometimes I feel that we are in a futuristic place and we still have our ancient ancestral thoughts begging us to follow old traditions. Fourteen year old were having babies, but if you know our history when a young girl was coming of age the women would take her and teach her how to maintain her family. Young men taught by the tribal elders how to hunt and take care of their families. Then our ancestors were transport to a land of concrete and we would have to adjust to this new environment. Its inhabitants, the rule required that you forget your roots and your soul and we did, and now our son's and daughter's are suffering, with no fear of death, and so they kill without conscience.

Warriors of the Neighborhood

An African Tradition of youth trying to wield their power, a
reminder that our history is not of here,
We have a story embedded in the blood,
We must follow our ancestor's way,
Though our lives are in concrete,
The origination is in the land of the Serengeti,
Where tribal elders take young warriors out, hunt, and fight
to establish male prowess,
Bringing it back for all to see his first,
Guided into manhood, made understood his
Responsibility to his family and his community,
To multiply his seed,
And then carry on the tradition,
The circle has been broken,
The young warrior is lost,
Practicing his tradition on concrete Streets
Fight his own likeness to establish a way,
No tribal elders to lead the way,
No hunt,
No family response,
No community to understand,
Just a lost warrior embedded concrete.

House of Females

My first day something strange, it was call higher school,
I was in a place laid back, I tried to be more like the females of classy, and they dressed with such coolness,
We celebrated moving up day,
It's when you are finally making it to the next level,
I was going to the eleventh grade and I finally could see the finish line in front of me,
But inside is turmoil and pain because, I am not sure what it is that I am supposed to do they make decisions with your life,
they teach me cooking and cleaning,
Something I do after school and on the weekend, I am in a single parent home, I want to work in an office, typing and filing, why can't they see?
I am sixteen and light a, can't they see?

I gage myself for those who look upon me, I have no real friend that would understand me, inside my head is my only friend Seth,
He advises me to ask for my curriculum to be changed then they said not this time, but if you think, you can do this next year, call me
Trader of a young soul

Demarco

An initiation trying to have his first, they chose me an angel waved her wings of distrust.
A chosen one for a special need, just to initiate my heart to his,
He failed to launch his love,
He felt ashamed,
He wanted my love, not my loving, he was of Latin descent,
and he was a smooth gang member, whom I adored,
He was quiet like the paws of a cat, taking me into him with his stare,
Creamery almadin casing, ocean waves striated across his mind,
Intense piercing eyes
And
A pleasant, alluring tone.
One that could have had my heart, a moment of truth he beseeched me not to inform anyone the secret there was not hatred, no respect, just the sharing of a friendly culture

School Walkout

A lunch discussion that led to a union walkout on school grounds, a protest of how our lunches were the worse, yet they wanted us to learn and become something great.
On dried hoagies and water please, we walked out the school and our brother from the adjacent school of the all male institution joins us because we are female, society.
Yet I found myself walking out of my classes to follow those who wanted more for us. We cheered for our ordacity, to literally protest our school; it was the first of many organize protest. At assembly, we were told that in us lies greatness, Auditorium sit in for better food, we were praised by our instructors for being challengers of things to make us better, I was proud of me that day, because I was apart something great, change.

Excerpt:

It was a massive snowstorm that left a foot and half of snow and I walked everywhere in my tall black boots that my mother bought me. I went to the store to get a couple of things that I needed when in the whitest snow was the blackest of men. He inquired my name and from there I fantasize my relationship with him. I tried to do all the proper things a lady should do, but the passion that I did not know how to control, got the best of me and many mistakes from my kind of thinking, led me down the wrong path.

Love abuse

You have no idea what love is about
All you know is a feeling.
Unfamiliar territory
All you know is that you must possess it, embrace it, and always want it in your life,
What is it that you love?
Its human, should you love with that magnitude, with that burning desire?
Love like the ocean massive and overwhelming, am I drowning?
A love so full that you feel you are suffocating,
You are the sender, what about the receiver?
Your object of great passion,
They are constantly looking for opening in this breathless environment that you created.
Then they escape into betrayal,
There is pain so deep, strong, that reality has no place in it, but sit quiet, subtract you from this hollow place.
Transfer that love to you, give it ya all, and move on because only you can deal with the ocean deep, pillow-suffocating love, and set that hawk free.

Teenage Mother

Deliberately I gave away my gift and he took it,

Happy that he was the first,

Then I am a mother

Positioned side my mother

Who was shocked by my conception?

I wanted something

That reflected him

A person who established him in me,

He walks a mile in disbelief

That he had did such a thing

That not only was I his baby's mother,

Someone else, in the south too.

Pain that would not go away,

Could not move it somewhere,

Starting small then becoming consistent,

How can I get the person out?

Fear helps me to be strong,

Then a person emerges

Slowly the pain disappears

I never saw her face because,

I went into a deep sleep,

Awaken to a new day,

A mother, a baby girl,

After seeing her beauty

Suddenly and without warning

Responsibility sets in

How will I set upon this Journey?

And its shores and be successful,

Something a teenage mother will have to know.

Hooky School

A mental health day once or twice year I am going downtown, shopping to find me something new, Yardley of London with the scent of lavender.

Then window-shopping and making sure that I come home on time, wondering through large department stores so young, yet beautiful.

The sales lady with her flawless makeup reminded me of the magazine of models who had the same beauty.

I was truant yet no one question this immature,

Sixteen year old being in the city so early in the day,

I had lunch at the five and dime.

Why would they call it Woolworth's?

Making sure I kept a vigil with the clock,

Catching the bus, exactly to the minute, to be on time.

Nervous stomach in hope they did not catch me,

A game of chance to see if I had the power, finally, my youngness is home. My mother did not see or ask,

Her friend scrutinizes, and it was cool

Discovery

A mirror revealing a stunning swan, never grasp that I was varying, fine thin hair materialize from my skin, I explore myself to see that I was changing, there was fondness of self. No longer wanting my mother to do my hair, changing from three braids to a French roll, my small frame could not fit clothes properly, yet I was gorgeous. While my body was changing, emotions were mounting, Retort intricate and mystified.

What was this sensation? Some day absolutely fabulous and others I just wanted to expire. No understanding of who I am, why or what I am to do, I made an autonomous choice for myself, tarnishing me. Guidance was self-taught, life was self-taught, I always said if I could go back with what I know at this very moment.
How I would change?

Aunt Sister

Beauty in darkness always appreciates

Mahogany smoothness at a century plus five

A stroke of her mind did not shake the

Will of her

She seeks the natural remedy

Leave those who are physicians of experiment

For they have no cure

Seek the herbs for healing

I touch her ebony arm amazed at its softness

Amazed at her fearlessness

At a one hundred and five

The only way the spirits could obtain her

They invade her slumber,

Where are you,

My sweet aunt sister….

Excerpt:

During my years of being young, I remember all my experiences like they were lessons, training me, teaching, letting me know that I would have a lot drama to go through on the world stage. I am a spiritual being having a human experience and it continues. What do you do with this experience I asked myself so many times? No one has ever come back from death to tell us what is like.

It has taken all this time to realize that I have been in control of my destiny in this life. The labels that we put on others or ourselves are just that, labels. They too are spiritual beings, and are trying to understand the human experience. Our knowledge or the acquiring of knowledge is for us to experience, to find out the outcome, and then whatever is needed later we use to boost us to a new learning level. From the day, we entered the world we are experiencing, growing in knowledge. Uplifting someone else, so that we can get to the next level, this happens from the beginning of time "from a wheel came a car" perspective. I watch and wonder where we are headed; hopefully, I will be going to the final experience, pure energy. Where I help to create new life forms, expand the universe travel through time and space.

 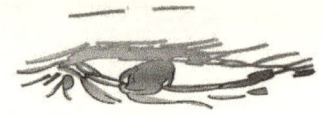

Grey Eyes

A life form that embraced life, it was the truth; this female had
no problem being bold and brash when it suited her mood.
Grey eyes had no illusion of life, no expectations from the
world; she was complete in her thoughts of what was needed.
Grey eyes, a penetrator of evil, when angry,
Yet she had the exquisiteness of a woman so fabulous.
Those in authority would partake of the pleasures of Grey eyes
She demanded compensation for her occasion,
Grey eyes made judges, doctors; lawyers terrified, all are
financially six figures
Grey eyes stop being an inhabitant experiencing the world and
started to participate in the humanity. Those eyes embraced
love,
Grey eyes, clone her being, and create a petite one whom fear
and loves her. Reality was always apart of a sonnet to her;
through the greyness of irises she saw it with passion, yet she
was a beautiful soul.
The devil came to her life and he disguised himself as a friend
but he stole a part of her being, she fought a valiant fight then
he took her last breath. All I know is
I will miss her humor, I will miss her eyes
I will miss a friend.
Those illustrious Grey eyes.

Excerpt:

My experience as a young woman led me to encounters of people that live their life deeply, emotionally, because of the environment they were brought up in, just like me, they tried to handle what is given to them the best way they could. I love people who live life, drug addicts, lesbians, gay people and prostitutes; I wanted to see how they live life, the lessons I learn from just talking to them, made me make some wise decisions and have kept me out of harms way. Here is my glass of champagne in honor of those who taught me what not to do.

Driven

From the beginning, I tried to control the sensitivity within, philosophy, stirring and proverbs, blunders designed, oh well, progress on time and time again.
Subtracting me empty power ,that I shared its love of appreciation, my power the orifice, the expressions motivate and share what I desire, and then unexpectedly silence, no one wishes my counsel, hoards it for me.
It is time to settle down, settle in, then doing what will take me to the next echelon,
And
Help move life forward,
Did you know we are believed to move beyond the speed of light?

Homeless

Pain was on the street one day, young, I inquisitive of his motives of being this way seen that the spirit that follow pleaded for my help, tall and elite with crimped hair that closely cut to his features, meaning he had seen a barber, did someone give him a gift of cut?

He was in halfway house, meaning one step from being on the streets forever, he lost his love and child, she wanted him to follow her dream, but he could not, so she locked the doors and sent him away.

Listening to pain is a dynamic in me,
A possible solution is understanding and a way to
Change the circumstance of his decision,
He expresses his desire to entertain, to be a voice on the radio,
so from my mouth are these words "Just do it!"
And oddly enough, he did!

A Extensive and Sandy Path

When I awoke to my being I was a diminutive person in side a building called me, unaware of the years and time that I would have to travel to make it to the point of understanding. While traveling to my history with twist and turns, I lived life and learned so much about those whom I encountered, they distrust me and so did I of them, believe that these words would be my epitaph, never did what I really wanted to do, because I was rushing head into life.

But my song goes "I am traveling a extensive and sandy path" and the only thing I really wanted is to do is move on to the next plane of existence.

Nina

The Empress Nina brought forth four kings and two queens,
A counselor of perception, truth, and the wisdom to
understand its meaning.
A canvasser of times past and reflection,
A constant being that poise the world with her Blackfoot
legacy from the mountains of West Virginia as the drum beats
Juanette,
Devotee of all life, even the ones whose existence were
discarded and mistreated,
Furnish them sanctuary,
Then preserve them for her,
Serenity in her life form so philosophical,
Her heart often enlighten to those who did partake of it.
Moments in time have passed and we mature with memories
of folks we encounter and still she is unchanged.
An Empress,
A Counselor,
A lover of life,
Nevertheless, "A benefactor of a loving spirit."

Excerpt:

Bless to meet someone who could help when I moved into the projects. The projects were dangerous and if you bragged about your life in anyway there were those who wanted nothing to make sure that you had nothing.

Project living

Twelve story house with twelve apartments on each floor. Families were housed here; people from all walks of life were given a place to live.

What made us all come here?
A husband abandoned his wife,
A person trying to escape abuse from a parent or a spouse,

Labeled and treated with disrespect,
Hustlers, whores, drug addicts, thieves and abusers,
Huddled together with people who were just thrown in the pot of Rosen, It wasn't choice, just chance, when you're at a project dance.

Human urination is sprayed by outside people who careless bout the children who frequent that hall or stair case,

The elevator opens to reveal that someone pulled their pants down, and left their feces for us to experience, with aromas that would make you take the stairs of open air.

Victims raped and molested by people, who did not, reside at our address yet, someone brought a small child to an empty apartment raped and through her body out the fifth floor window; He was the Childs family friend.

Then you try to make the best of bad situation, dressing your children for school that is only across the street, when the elevator is broken for the millionth time, they must take the steps.

On the tenth floor a body lay in the damp stillness with an ice pick in his chest.

The reward of a devastated child, no school, lets go somewhere so that we can remove that image from their mind.

Hustler female

A hustler in female form, who would shake you down with a vengeance,
Her laughs fake, as she schemes against you,
She had no acquaintances, just lovers who meant naught to her,
She helps people rob and pillage, cheating young thieves out of their bounty,
Spirit knew her well,
Brazen female whose house the spirit sat a blaze,
People discussed her misfortune yet happy that everything vanished.
Give her your drugs and she will sell them, and then dupe you out of the money,
Give her your money and she spends it, never ask her where it is,
Give her your life, and then she will give them a room to torture and kill you,
Help her to steal and she will let the law incarcerate you,
She will forget your existence.
Her roots were of Arkansas,
Are their black folk in that place?
If yes, then are they like her,
Close the doors and lock them,
Nail down everything that moves.

Excerpt:

I had to really work out who I had become, inside I had a mission to become something better than I had become. Project living taught how mindsets of the inhabitants work. A lesson greatly appreciated by me.

No Food Just mouths

An organization to help they say, but the truth is in complacency, to remain under their power, rations must last, but the mouths are hungry, mouths express desire, while yanking the sequence of approval and dangle it before all in the system," is it now?" we ask! Not today, "is it today?" Soon, refrigerators hollow, with the whine of a motor humming, scrape the icy snow, inside freezers because there is nothing else.

One egg in the tray, and no grits, not butter, but not even margarine, counting the change in the purse, only a dollar,
In sofa frame, we almost have two, keep looking, we are going to get a loaf of bread, one dollars worth of bologna, a dollar of cheese, and a loaf of bread. Maybe if we continue to search, we can have some cool aide, damn no sugar!

No don't borrow, then we will owe, keep busy, go to sleep and wake to another dawn, stomach growling, awakening with an attitude. Knowing the next resonance you will hear, is the mouths saying,
"Mommy I am hungry."

East River Drive

On foot with nature, solitary, I seek, a drive of cars across from the stream wandering from estuary extensive and cavernous, I situate my carcass amid the blades of grass.

Scrutinizing huge bee's that seek out nectarine flowers so sweet, in the distance were a populace enjoying the breeze while others speculate about what they perceive.

With pen in furnish I inscribe the verse East River a place of serenity for me.

I walked seeking the path and discover it surrounded by the trees triumph the sky, with great birds overhead and pebbles under foot. Spring water lucid swathe the rocks spotless of debris,

Yet, there is no fear of what is ahead,
Greeting from those who have taken the path
And
Experience the river on the east.

Holiday Nightmares

Holiday's don't stop because you are a mother,
Stressed to make your little ones happy,
You're stress out on how to handle it,
 You only have two dollars,
And three children,
Father who is sporting silk and gators,
While children are dressed in hand me downs,
Scrutinizing lies on television of Santa generous gifts,
While the truth is you have no money,
No gifts and you have no idea who Santa is,
Santa to young minds is a spirit that they think
Comes with happiness and joy and don't forget the toy,
When all my kids are grown, then my nightmare is over,
Get rid of festivity and live life,
Hassle free and feeling fine.

Excerpt:
When I wrote this line I keep hearing the voice of a man in my mind
Free at last, free at last.

Dark Stairway

Get ready walking into a building of blackness in the stairwell,
something could be waiting in the corners as I climb to the
eleventh floor, finding my flashlight I keep a vigil of the
corners of whom may be hiding and lurking for me.
The concrete stairs are hard and dirty with the stench of
urination, a sudden opening of a door on a floor reveals
nothing but piping and so you breathe a sight of relief.
A child launches himself out into the darkness without fear,
He sees and acknowledges your name while moving his body
at light speed toward the next floor,
It is three in the morning and he is nine,
His mother is in a drunken stupor unknowing of him missing,
Finally, the seventh floor I take a deep breath and smell seems
to be piss, and shit and something ungodly.
Laughter is heard nearby,
Then I move up to the next floor,
Loud music heard there is party going on!
With one deep breath I make it to my floor,
Only to see the door of the elevator comes open
A neighbor greets me with a drunken slur
In my mind, what am I doing here?

Haven

A man who adopted by a family that he needed,
His life was to be a writer,
Yet, women who like his sex held him hostage,
They gave him children,
For me he was too easy some say,
He was a country boy with a nose that you could run through,
His body limp and frail,
And yet he belong no place,
Finally alcohol introduce him to itself,
Then he lost his way,
"There has never been a family!" He cried,
Never became a writer,
Never understood my life,
Then he faded away.

Excerpt:

The were many men of foreign descent that passed my way, But this one brought happiness in my life. He was tall and dark, and wore woven sweaters, and trousers that were gracing his finesse.
He was only here for the education, and the understanding of our culture, all the while his social skills were outstanding. He brought humor to events and functions that grace our presence.

Oboe

An effigy of bronze that escort me in the night sky,
He was an instrument of a Ugandan Prince, who was here to achieve his education, my imagination was so unsure of his intentions, yet I wanted his closeness to my heart.

A Young lion confident of his approach, through multitude of society parties, his tall illumination towering above all else "I see you, he say!" but, how could he not, we all could see him too.

His brownness was different from the chocolate in
America it was so clear, yet it had a unique layer,
I met him, only to see him once,
He returns to Uganda,
 Was he the son of Amine?

                                                  What tribal house was he?
Prince of Uganda…

Piccadilly

Eight females require an evening on the town, a guild we all go. Music blaring, more bounce to the ounce and the big butt sisters has no problem, working it out.
The DJ is in concert playing my song tonight.
A nightspot lit flooring;
Brothers trying to unearth a woman to siesta,
And two bars to get your drink on,
Yet around the wall were the people who hung out
Together,
Then the light comes on and you are awaken from
Your party-slumber,
Last call for alcohol,
Yet, you are not finished partying,
"Let find the after hours spot."

Excerpt: The Evaluation

Listen to your being. You have much to say. . This has been a learning experience for me. I remembered so much about my life. I always cried as a baby because everyone that I really loved, left me, abandoned me. I could never get into a relationship that meant anything because I was scared of being abandoned.

Being human in this world was devastating because I just did not know what to do. I am a spirit having a human experience. I guess you say what does that mean. Well it means that I lost my father before I could etch him in my psyche, so I experience separation anxiety. My mother left me because she was going through her own experience and she did not know how to deal with her life and me at the same time. I also experience neglect and it manifests itself in the form of distrust of people.

My grandmother gave me her love so unconditionally that I have never experience that kind of love since she left the planet, and I will never experience it again. When she left, I just bottled up my feeling and thoughts and said that I would not engage my heart in that kind of love ever again. I fell in love with a man who did not have any inkling about love. He has to live a certain type of drama so he did not know anything about loving and caring for a woman.

Then my children are a next generation of women that are trying to deal with my way of raising them. They too are spirits having a human experience.

Wondering about why they were brought to this place without their permission. I could take a moment and explain that the reason they are here they are apart of the universal order of things. That they were apart of asteroids, comets or something that penetrated the earth millions of years ago and from that one amoeba, they were created until we have become the beings we are today.

Yes, I am deep when it comes to thinking about the existence of us. So, what will we evolve into if we are going through this universe or all the universes? I have no idea, all I know is that I am looking forward to my spirit moving on into other realms and taking the knowledge that I have right now into another existence.

I hope that I will be among life forces that are intelligent and are looking for ways to be creative in their mode of existence.

For those religious and political people who are thinking that her elevator has not went to the top. Hear this, you experience this life and you may feel all warm and fuzzy but soon all the minds that are asleep will awaken one day, god help you. The existence of Heaven or Hell is something on this plain of existence, it is understandable, I guess it is what a person who is experiencing this life needs. I do not need heaven or hell; I need experience in intelligent beings that could teach me how to live in these universes. "That's all!

Eleth

An innovative narration is,

In the mist

Hence

There will be

A

Re-visit.

www.ingramcontent.com/pod-product-compliance
Lightning Source LLC
Chambersburg PA
CBHW032004080426
42735CB00007B/504